Cover illustration: An SR-71 Blackbird accelerates in full afterburner into the sunset. (Author)

1. TR-1A 01067 on a company test flight near Palmdale. Optical sensors are probably installed for this flight (note the clear opening in the Q-bay). (Lockheed)

WARBIRDS ILLUSTRATED NO. 24
US Spyplanes
ERIK SIMONSEN

ARMS AND ARMOUR PRESS

Introduction

Published by Arms and Armour Press Limited,
Link House, West Street, Poole, Dorset
BH15 1LL.

Distributed in the USA by Sterling Publishing Co.
Inc., 2 Park Avenue, New York, NY 10016.

Distributed in Australia by Capricorn Link
(Australia) Pty. Ltd., P.O. Box 665, Lane Cove,
New South Wales 2066, Australia.

First published 1985. Reprinted 1987.

British Library Cataloguing in Publication Data:
Simonsen, Erik
U.S. spyplanes – (Warbirds illustrated; 24)
1. Aerial reconnaissance – United States – History –
Pictorial works
I. Title   II. Series
358.4′5′0973   UG765.U6

ISBN 0-85368-626-2

Edited and designed by Roger Chesneau; printed
and bound in Italy.

Ever since the first aerial photograph was taken, from a military observation balloon, commanders have been fascinated with this capability, and over the years systems have evolved into extremely sophisticated devices, capable of gathering all forms of data, from low-level tactical observation to Earth-orbit, high-resolution photography. Today's satellite systems afford facilities for very high quality elint (electronics intelligence) and photographic reconnaissance, but, complementing the data returned from space, that collected by the manned aircraft is still vital, and the need for immediate, accurate information has led to the development of stable and flexible reconnaissance platforms known as 'spyplanes'.

We will, in this volume, only glimpse the strategic reconnaissance story. Missions are usually carried out under a cloak of extreme secrecy by a single aircraft. No weapons are carried nor payloads delivered, only the probing eyes of photo-optical systems or the invisible impulses of electronic sensors. Even when a particular mission is successful, there can be no disclosure or claim of recognition. The need for policy makers to have an immediate assessment of a global 'hot spot' or to accumulate the information necessary to determine long-term strategy depends on reconnaissance capabilities. Within this realm we will look at several of the truly amazing aircraft that have been produced to meet this need.

Many aircraft specifically developed to carry out a strategic reconnaissance role have become 'classics' and have performed well beyond what could originally have been imagined. In this respect, special recognition must go to the creative design genius of Clarence 'Kelly' Johnson of the Lockheed-California Company: his name and successful futuristic aircraft are synonymous. It is difficult to believe that the Lockheed U-2, first flown in 1955, is, in the form of the U-2R/TR-1, still contributing today. As far as we know, the U-2 has gone back into production at least three times since its inception. The F-12 series of high-performance Mach 3+ aircraft was originally developed as a programme of advanced interceptors. The design finally evolved into the SR-71, which is featured heavily in this volume. Strategic Air Command keeps 'an unspecified number' of Blackbirds on flight status and another 'unspecified number' in flyable storage. They are rotated in and out as demand arises and budgets allow. Although the airframe itself reportedly acquires strength through age, many subsystems have to be replaced on a continuing basis.

Unlike that of the U-2, the SR-71's tooling was destroyed after the initial production run. Perhaps this tells us something; perhaps more efficient tooling methods for a follow-on aircraft were being considered many years ago. In some areas the cloak of mystery is being gently lifted, but we can only speculate about the future. For now, we must study what we have.

For their assistance with photographs for this volume, special thanks go to Bob Ferguson, Lockheed-California Co.; Jim Goodall; John Andrews; Lt. Col. John Alexander USAF, Offutt AFB; and Nancy Lovato (NASA/Dryden FRF).

Erik Simonsen

◄2
2. A low-angle photograph of the YF-12A gives an impressive view of the radome and chine running back from the spherical white infra-red detectors. The pods below the engine nacelles contained high-speed cameras to record weapons separation during tests. (Lockheed)

▲ 3

▲ 4 ▼ 5

3. The U-2 prototype (Article 341) awaits its first flight beneath the desert sun and approaching thunderstorms. This is one of the few photographs of aircraft 001. (Lockheed)

4. Newly painted in overall black, U-2B/N803X displays its clean lines at Lockheed's Palmdale facility. When Gary Powers' U-2 was shot down over the Soviet Union on 1 May 1960, the Soviets fired a large number of SAMs along his track. They even managed to shoot down some of their MiG fighters that were trailing the U-2 at lower altitudes: at one point, Warsaw Pact troops converged on a descending parachute only to find a Soviet MiG pilot. (Lockheed)

5. Clarence L. 'Kelly' Johnson with two of his most successful designs. The U-2 and F-104 are a tribute to his genius. (Lockheed)

6. U-2B/N809X during a test flight for the Central Intelligence Agency (CIA). All Agency aircraft received a temporary number during testing and training within US borders. Note the extended airbrake. (Lockheed)

7. U-2A 66701 flies over the mountains near Palmdale during the test programme; this particular photograph is not often seen. The aircraft was subsequently converted into U-2B/U-2C configurations and is now on display at the Offutt AFB/SAC Museum. (Lockheed)

8. The clean lines and high-aspect ratio wing are evident in this view of U-2A 66708. (Lockheed)

9. U-2A 66708 again, showing unit citation, in the early natural metal scheme. Note the reflection beneath the port horizontal stabilizer. (Lockheed)

10. Two early-model U-2s, 66701 (in starboard bank) and 66722 (with a rotating optical sensor fitted and rear-view mirror removed) fly in formation over the Mojave Desert. (Lockheed)

11. Its well-known 'Smokey Joe' tail insignia visible, 66722 joins up on number 66701 once again. Both aircraft participated in many test flight programmes, including HICAT, which investigated high-altitude, clear-air turbulence. (Lockheed)

12. Slightly soft in quality, this photograph of U-2D 66721 is nevertheless quite rare. The vertical sensor can be seen just aft of the cockpit. (USAF)

10▲

11▲ 12▼

▲13

▲14

13. The two-tone grey scheme developed for European U-2 duties is shown in this study of U-2C 66714 on the flight line at Davis-Monthan AFB, Arizona. This particular aircraft was repainted black in 1979 and is now on permanent display at Beale AFB, California. (Goodall Collection)

14. A rare view of operations during the Vietnam War at Udorn AB in Northern Thailand, showing a U-2C of the 100th SRW preparing for a mission over 'the north' in 1968. (Author's Collection)

15. The F-12/A-12 series of aircraft line up for a rare photo session during the 'High Point' test programme. The two-seat trainer is in the No. 2 position. (Andrews via Goodall)

16. A 1968 NASA/Landsat view of the Groom Lake test facility (Watertown Strip/'The Ranch'), which is located approximately 100 miles north-west of Las Vegas, Nevada. Most ultra-secret work has now moved on to two other facilities. Note the B-52 on the flight apron in the centre of the photograph. (NASA via Andrews)

▼15

16▶

17. The only in-flight photograph released of an A-12 (06932). The A-12 was a single-seat aircraft and performed Agency (CIA) missions, during which it carried no national markings. (Lockheed)

18. The bare metal and black prototype YF-12A (06934) on the ramp at the Groom Lake test facility. (Lockheed)

19. A striking view of an early YF-12A. The aircraft would not be out of place in a *Star Wars* film – imagine the visual impact during the early 1960s! (Goodall Collection)

20. The prototype YF-12A reveals its profile high above the Nevada Desert. The photo-documentation markings appear to be interchangeable. As in this photograph, the horizon features in YF-12 prints are sometimes airbrushed out. (Lockheed)

21. Kelly Johnson with the third YF-12A (06936). Johnson, the head of Lockheed's Advanced Development Projects (ADP), or 'Skunk Works', designed the P-38, P-80, F-104 and U-2 as well as the Blackbird series. (Lockheed)

19 ▲

20 ▼

21 ▼

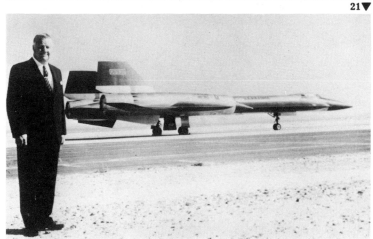

22. An excellent overhead view of YF-12A 06936 early in the interceptor test programme. This aircraft was lost as a result of a hydraulic failure during a landing approach at Edwards on 24 June 1971. (Lockheed)

23. Another view of 06936 displaying its graceful lines. The YF-12A was 101ft 8in in length and had a wing span of 55ft 7in. The reconfigured chine allowed for the installation of the Hughes ASG-18 fire control radar. (Lockheed)

24. The A-12/YF-12A provided invaluable flight-test data for the follow-on reconnaissance platform, the SR-71. Note the insignia commemorating the aircraft's achievements and the Hughes AIM-47A air-to-air missile. (Goodall Collection)

25. An early 1960s view of the YF-12A, showing the aircraft's dagger-like profile. Edwards AFB is in the background. (Lockheed)

▲22　▼23

▲26

26. The first YF-12A being readied for a test flight during the early 1960s interceptor programme. The 60-degree sweep of the 'double-delta' wing is readily apparent. (Lockheed)

27. A publicity photograph showing a crew approaching a YF-12A and carrying their air-conditioning units. These units provide a comfortable temperature within the cumbersome flying suits until the crewmen plug themselves into the aircraft systems. Note the absence of support equipment. (Pratt & Whitney)

28. A YF-12A pulls in next to its chase plane, allowing a good view of the centreline ventral fin. The fin folds down as the landing gear retracts. (Lockheed)

29. Its power at idle, YF-12A 06935 settles in for a landing on the main runway at Edwards AFB. The huge delta wing creates 'ground effect', allowing for smooth landings. Note the Presidential unit citation above the tail number. (Lockheed)

30. The J-58 (military designation) or JT11D-20B development engine is in itself a magnificent technological feat – it was the first triple-sonic rated powerplant capable of sustaining long periods of flight in afterburner. At speed and at altitude, the inlets and exhaust nozzles actually produce about 90 per cent of the thrust. (Pratt & Whitney)

▼27

28▲

29▲ 30▼

▲ 31

▲ 32

31. The ramjet D-21 (GTD-21B) drone was launched from a modified A-12 or M-12 mother plane. Aircraft 06940 is shown, with a GTD-21B aboard; note the intake cover (the exhaust cover is not visible). Continuing problems, and a fatality on 30 July 1966, led to the termination of this launch method. (Lockheed)

32. Launched from a B-52 pylon, the D-21 was accelerated with the assistance of a booster attached to the underside of the drone. The high speed was necessary to ignite the ramjet engine. (Lockheed)

33. Basking in the desert sun, seventeen GTD-21B drones enjoy retirement, July 1983. Originally codenamed 'Oxcart', the D-21s were launched most successfully utilizing the B-52. (Knowles via Goodall)

34. A close-up view of a D-21, showing the inlet and bypass doors. (Knowles via Goodall)

35. The ramjet D-21 is thought to have flown reconnaissance missions in high-threat areas above Mach 4.5 at over 100,000ft. It could map out air defence threats or produce false radar images ahead of manned reconnaissance flights. (Knowles via Goodall)

▼ 33

34▲   35▼

▲36 ▼37

38▲

39▲

36. The RB-57 was developed to fill the requirement for a reconnaissance aircraft that could carry more payload than the U-2 and provide for a two-man crew. (General Dynamics)
37. The first RB-57F, having just received its J-60-P9 powerplants. The nacelles for the J-60s are easily removed in order that pods or external stores may be attached. (General Dynamics)
38. General Dynamics modified the B-57 into RB-57 configuration with cost-effectiveness in mind; tooling developed under the B-58 Hustler programme was utilized. (Author's Collection)
39. RB-57F 928, with NASA/DOE (Department of Energy) markings. The RB-57F was well suited to its role of high-altitude sampling of radioactive particles. (Goodall)
40. A good view of the RB-57F wing. The 122ft span was almost double the fuselage length and may be compared to the 64ft span of the original B-57. (General Dynamics)

40▼

▲41

41. A rare head-on view of the first SR-71 (17950) before it acquired its all-black scheme. (Pratt & Whitney)

42, 43. Differences between nose chines: the YF-12A is on the left and the SR-71A on the right. The SR-71A has a fuselage length of 107ft 5in. (Lockheed)

44. A good view of the blended-body forward chine (extending over approximately 40 per cent of the aircraft's length) of the SR-71. This particular nose fitting contains no special equipment for surveillance. (Author)

45. Inlet and spike detail on aircraft 17960. Critical inlet control, throughout the flight envelope, is necessary for optimum performance. (Author)

▼42

▼43

44▲   45▼

46. During October 1973, observers at Beale AFB caught a rare view of two SR-71s in formation, headed for Griffis AFB, New York. Blackbirds have flown in formation at supersonic speeds within 500ft of each other, with no apparent problem. (USAF via Goodall)

47. A good view of aircraft 17962 prior to joining up with a KC-135Q. The SR-71 can cover a distance of 2,000 miles in just over an hour while surveying 100,000 square miles of surface territory. (Lockheed)

48. NASA YF-12A 06935 taxis out to the main runway at Edwards AFB, March 1979. (Author)

49. Racing down the runway with each J-58 producing over 30,000lb of thrust, a YF-12A nears lift-off. Typical take-off speed was approximately 200kts and runway roll 5,400ft. (Author)

50. Silhouetted against the desert mountains, a NASA F-104G chase plane and a NASA YF-12A prepare for take-off. (Author)

▲46 ▼47

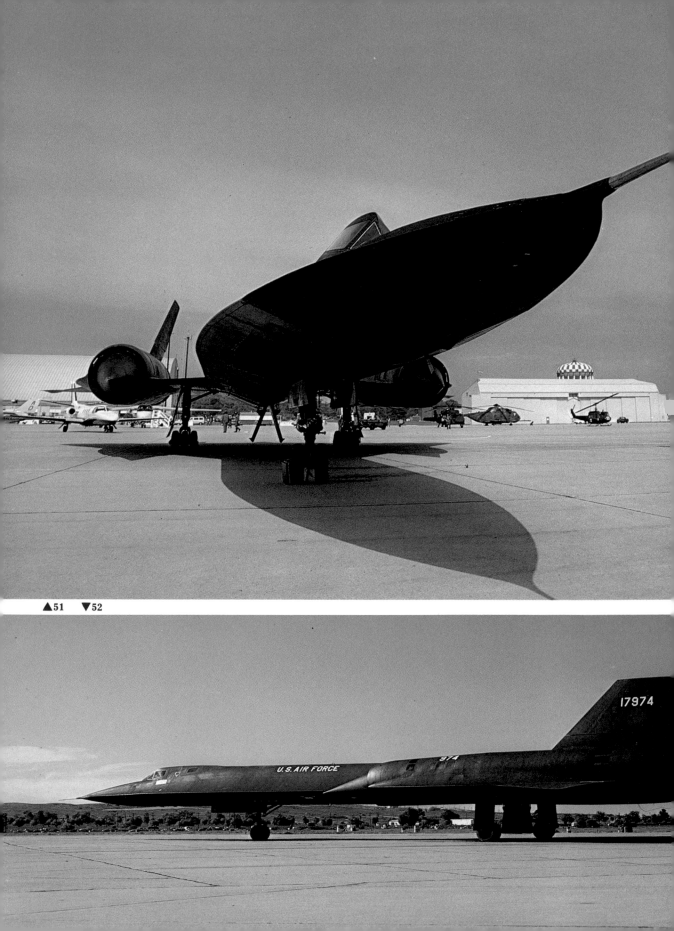

▲51 ▼52

53▲

54▲

51. A wide-angle view of the nose chine of the SR-71. This aircraft was photographed during a visit to Andrews AFB, Maryland. (Author)
52. A good profile view of SR-71 17974 taxiing out to the main runway at March AFB, California, during November 1981. (Author)
53. A Lockheed SR-71 accelerates in afterburner over Southern California. (Author)
54. A NASA U-2C prepares for an engine run-up test at Ames Research Center, Moffett Field, California. (Author)
55. A U-2R with pogos attached moves on to the main ramp at Andrews AFB, Maryland. (Author)

55 ▼

▲56 ▼57

56. This view of an SR-71 being towed to the hangar area at Andrews AFB illustrates the new low-visibility markings now applied to the Blackbirds. Aircraft 17960 received its new scheme during May 1984. (Author)

57. With afterburners glowing, an SR-71 accelerates rapidly. The SR-71 is heavier and has a longer range than the YF-12A, although both utilize the same engine. (Author)

58. An SR-71 poses with operational aircraft at Beale AFB, California during the late 1960s; this SR-71 (17970) was lost in an air refuelling accident on 17 June 1970. The T-38 is similar in handling characteristics to the SR-71 at subsonic speeds. At this time the North American Hound Dog missile (seen on the B-52 pylons) was still on the USAF inventory. (USAF)

59. Aircraft 66953 was rebuilt into a two-seat trainer (U-2CT) during 1972, and the rigorous flight training programme for U-2 pilots was thereby helped immensely. (Lockheed)

60. The majestic U-2R in flight over snow-capped mountains. For some reason the tail number has been airbrushed out on this photograph. Note the tail warning sensor on the trailing edge of the starboard wing. (USAF)

58▲

59▲   60▼

▲61

▲62   ▼63

61. A U-2R at rest at Beale AFB, California, during a post-flight inspection. The 'howdah' sunshade is in position. (Goodall)

62. A close-up view of the TR-1's cockpit and intake area, taken during an August 1982 visit to March AFB, California. At that time this aircraft had accumulated only 7 flying hours. The fan in the cockpit is used as a demister. (Author)

63. U-2R 10337 taxis up to the flight line at Andrews AFB, Maryland. Note the KC-10A landing in background. (Author)

64. A U-2R in landing configuration turns in on final approach to Beale AFB, California. The U-2 is an extremely difficult aircraft to land – and is more so after a tiring, long-endurance mission. (Goodall)

65. U-2EP-X 10339 soars over the ocean, 1973. The Navy's Ocean Surveillance Patrol programme was developed to test various new sensors and their effectiveness at sea, including RCA X-band radar, real-time monitoring devices and a forward-looking infra-red radar system. (Lockheed)

64▲   65▼

▲66

66. Ground support personnel check out NASA YF-12A 06935 prior to engine start. (Author)

67. NASA YF-12A 06935 and YF-12C 06937 in formation during a test programme. Aircraft 06935 is carrying the 'Coldwall experiment' on hard points beneath its fuselage. The hollow cylinder, 3.04m in length, was used to study the effects of aerodynamic heating on nitrogen-cooled equipment. Note the Lockheed 'skunk' on 06935's ventral fin. (NASA)

68. Detail of NASA YF-12A 06935, showing the 'skunk' and crew signatures on its ventral fin. These and the NASA markings were removed prior to the aircraft's last flight to the Air Force Museum

on 7 November 1979. (Author)

69. NASA conducted extensive test flights utilizing two YF-12As and a YF-12C. The information-gathering was directed at structural/performance research, stability/control aerodynamics and biomedical research. Both NASA and Air Force crews participated in the aeronautical research programme, which lasted from May 1970 to November 1979. (NASA)

70. YF-12C 06937 (actually SR-71 17951) cruises over the Sierra Mountains during a test flight. Data gathered during the NASA/Air Force programme would be applied to future supersonic aircraft. (NASA)

▼67

68▲

69▲ 70▼

▲71 ▼72   ▼73

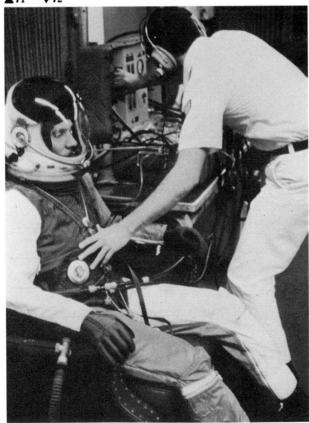

71. The High Temperature Loads Calibration Facility at Edwards AFB contains a structure that can simulate temperatures encountered at Mach 2.5 plus. The effects of sustained temperatures up to 750°F were tested on the YF-12A fuselage, as the structure encompassed the aircraft. (NASA)

72. An SR-71 crew member receives assistance from a Physiological Support Division (PSD) technician. The crew must breathe pure oxygen for 30 minutes before take-off in order to purge their systems of nitrogen. (USAF)

73. Intense concentration shows on the face of an SR-71 pilot as he prepares for an operational mission. The parameters in which the Blackbird flies leave little margin for error. (USAF)

74. PSD technicians remain with the flight crew until they are plugged into the aircraft. (Goodall)

75. Moment of ignition! Within its own specialized hangar at Beale AFB, an SR-71 starts No. 2 engine. Because of the high flashpoint of the JP-7 (a lighted match will not ignite it), triethylborane (TEB) is injected into the engine once the air turbine starter has built up RPMs. Afterburners are also ignited in this manner. (Goodall)

▲76

▲77 ▼78

76. With a snappy salute from a ground crew member, an SR-71 taxis out, ready to go. Note the dark strip under the nose, indicating an area for sensor equipment. (USAF)

77. An SR-71B trainer above a remote area near the California/ Nevada border. The raised second cockpit was integrated into an existing SR-71A airframe to produce this much-utilized trainer. (Lockheed)

78. Produced from salvaged parts (including the rear half of YF-12A 06934), SR-71B 17981 cruises above Northern California. The SR-71B features nacelle ventral fins to balance the raised

cockpit. Note the mid-fuselage structure under unusual lighting conditions. (Lockheed)

79. A rare formation of famous spyplanes: SR-71 17955, operating out of Lockheed-Palmdale, joins up with a tactical reconnaissance U-2R over the Mojave Desert. (Lockheed)

80. Delicate hook-up with a KC-135Q. On 26 April 1971 an SR-71 utilizing a series of air-to-air refuellings flew 15,000 miles in 10½ hours. The flight won for the crew the coveted Mackay Trophy. (Goodall Collection)

▲81

81. The Lockheed-operated SR-71, 17955, hooks up with a KC-135Q. A special communications secure-link (enabling the duo to maintain radio silence) is one of the features of the Q-model tanker. (Lockheed)

82. A large, bright orange drag chute helps with the wear and tear on the brake system. The chute is jettisoned at 60mph to avoid entanglement with the aircraft. (USAF)

82 ▼

▲83

83. Aircraft 17977 overran the runway at Beale AFB on 10 October 1968. The crew escaped. (Marysville Appeal: Democrat via Goodall)

84. The SR-71 is capable of speeds beyond Mach 3 (over 2,000mph) – a velocity of over 3,100 feet per second, which is faster than the muzzle velocity of a 30.6 rifle bullet. (Lockheed)

85. An overhead view of aircraft 19755, with drag chute trailing, landing at Lockheed's Palmdale facility. (Lockheed)

86. SR-71 17962 springs off the runway at Beale AFB, California. On 27–28 July 1976, two SR-71 aircraft, flying at 2,193.6mph, recaptured the world's record for speed over a straight course, and set a new absolute/class sustained altitude record of 85,068.99ft. Note the white-cross markings for verification/tracking purposes. (USAF)

▼84

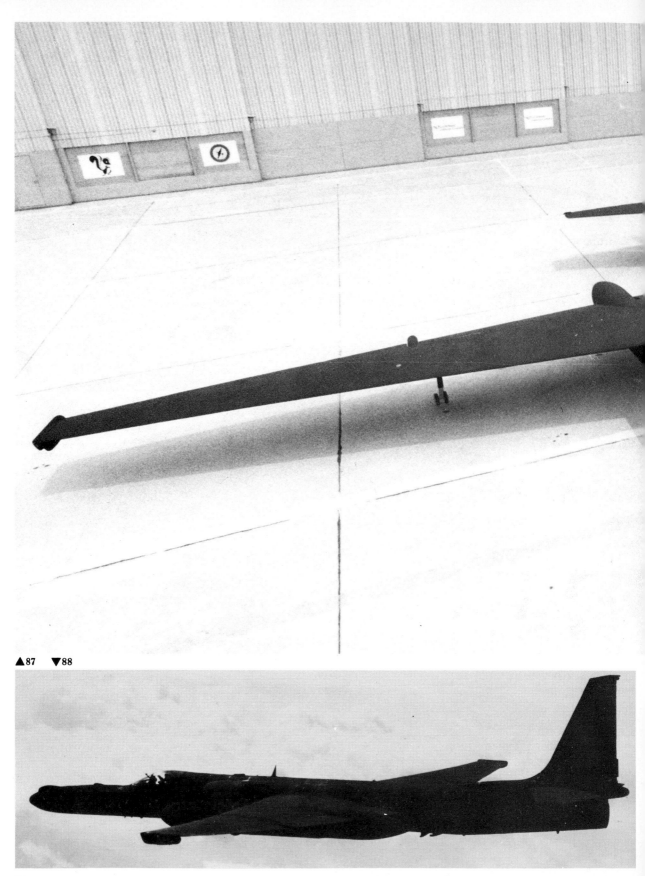

▲87 ▼88

42

89 ▼

87. The first TR-1A, 01066, just prior to roll-out at Lockheed's Palmdale facility. The TR-1A was designed for a tactical reconnaissance role and is currently testing the Advanced Synthetic Aperture Radar System (ASARS), built by Hughes. (Lockheed)

88. A good view of one of the more unusual nose extensions on U-2R 10336. Under a 1977 contract, Lockheed is now testing the Precision Emitter Location Strike System (PLSS). (USAF)

89. Advanced hemispherical warning devices (RHAW) are installed on the TR-1A. Aircraft 01068 is seen here at March AFB, California, one month before heading over to the 1982 Farnborough Air Show. (Author)

▲90

90. The TR-1A will provide NATO allies with all-weather, day or night battlefield surveillance. Capable of carrying nearly two tons of sensors (optical/elint), the TR-1A has a range of more than 3,000 miles (4,800km). (Lockheed)

91. A view showing the much larger wing area of the TR-1; this aircraft is 40 per cent larger than the older U-2 models. For some reason the tail number has been obliterated. (Lockheed)

▼91

92. An SR-71 over Southern California. The chine provides excellent lift. (Author)

93. SR-71 17960, bearing new low-visibility markings, begins its climb out. (Author)

94. (Next spread) Ground crew at March AFB, California, make the final pre-flight checks on an SR-71 that looks anxious to go. (Author)

95. A NASA F-104G chase plane pursues a YF-12A down the main runway at Edwards AFB, California. (Author)

96. An impression of a future high-altitude reconnaissance aircraft. (Author)

97. Under a gloomy sky, an RC-135U lands at Offutt AFB, Nebraska. The RC-135s, extensively modified and packed with electronic 'black boxes', perform a variety of elint (electronics intelligence), sigint (signals intelligence) and comint (communications intelligence) missions. (Goodall)

98. The Side-Looking Airborne Radar (SLAR) bulge is evident near the nose of this visiting RC-135 at March AFB in August 1982. (Author)

99. Through fog and cloud cover, Synthetic Aperture Radar can provide detailed 3-dimensional radar-generated imagery. (Author)

97▲

98▲　　99▼

▲ 100

100. The RC-135U in the elint role will lock on to and record specific frequencies as the aircraft patrols well away from unfriendly borders. (Goodall)

101. RC-135s lined up at Offutt AFB, Nebraska. Variants of the C-135 are utilized for all types of Air Force missions, including command and control 'looking glass' reconnaissance, long-range weather reconnaissance and various elint missions. (Goodall)

102. The first production TR-1B two-seat trainer, over Northern California. (Lockheed)

103. A good view of the TR-1B's raised cockpit, which provides visibility for the instructor in this dual-controlled trainer version. (Goodall)

▼ 101

▲104

104. With snow-capped mountains in the background, a TR-1B soars during a test flight. (Lockheed)

105. An extremely clear photograph of aircraft 17964. The SR-71 is practically a flying fuel tank, with a capacity for approximately 12,000 gallons. The fuel acts as a heat-sink for the aircraft, and a nitrogen inerting system is used to reduce the fire hazard. (Lockheed)

105▼

U.S. AIR FORCE

▲106 ▼107

108▲

106. With the 'Bunny' insignia on its tail, the 'Rapid Rabbit' heads out on a training mission. A pre-cut mission tape is inserted into the Automatic Navigation System (ANS) before each flight, providing for precise manoeuvres during the entire flight envelope. (Lockheed)

107. The SR-71 performs elint missions as well as photographic reconnaissance flights. The side-looking features of both systems give excellent slant range resolution. (Lockheed)

108. A NASA U-2C/709 in an early paint scheme. The Ames Research Center at Moffett Field, California, has two U-2C aircraft and a new ER-2 (Earth Resource) variant of the TR-1A. (NASA)

109. The NASA ER-2 provides an excellent platform for various scientific instruments. The U-2Cs and ER-2 collect data on such environmental features as forestry, flood damage, crop disease and water resources. (Lockheed)

109▼

▲110   ▲111 ▼112

113 ▲

110. The cockpit of the NASA U-2C/709 is quite small. The drift sight for ground tracking is above the yoke. (Goodall)
111. The optical ports of the NASA ER-2 Q-bay hatch. (Goodall)
112. A NASA U-2C in the Ames Research Center hangar. The tail section has been removed and the J-75-P-13B engine is visible on

the right. (Author)
113. Lockheed technicians check out NASA U-2C prior to engine run-up. The Q-bay hatch has been removed. (Author)
114. NASA U-2C/708 during major overhaul at Ames Research Center. (Goodall)

114 ▼

▼115

◀116
117▲

115. The ER-2 undergoing a manufacturer's test flight before delivery to NASA in early 1982. (Lockheed)

116. The ER-2 is able to carry up to 3,000lb of scientific instruments. On one occasion, an earlier U-2C actually collected 4,500,000,000-year-old dust from a comet at 65,000ft. (Lockheed)

117. From 1982 to 1983 several SR-71s went through a transitional low-visibility scheme. All white lettering was removed and national insignia in red stencil, with 'USAF' in red on the rudders, were applied on a few aircraft. (Goodall)

▲ 118

118. Awaiting final taxi on to the main runway at Beale, aircraft 17973 shows the interim red stencil national insignia. (Goodall)
119. The SR-71 is now appearing with a red tail number only and no national markings. Here, 17960 performs a high-speed pass. (Author)
120. SR-71 17960, in low-visibility scheme. Note the fuel dump at the rear of the aircraft. Fuel balance is critical for centre of gravity control and optimum efficiency. (Author)
121. A close view of the tail section reveals smaller numbers in red. There is no technical reason given for the change – just a standardization with the U-2R/TR-1A fleet. (Author)
122. Even the crew escape/rescue information lettering is devoid of bright colours and is flat red. (Author)

▼ 119

▼ 120

121▲ 122▼

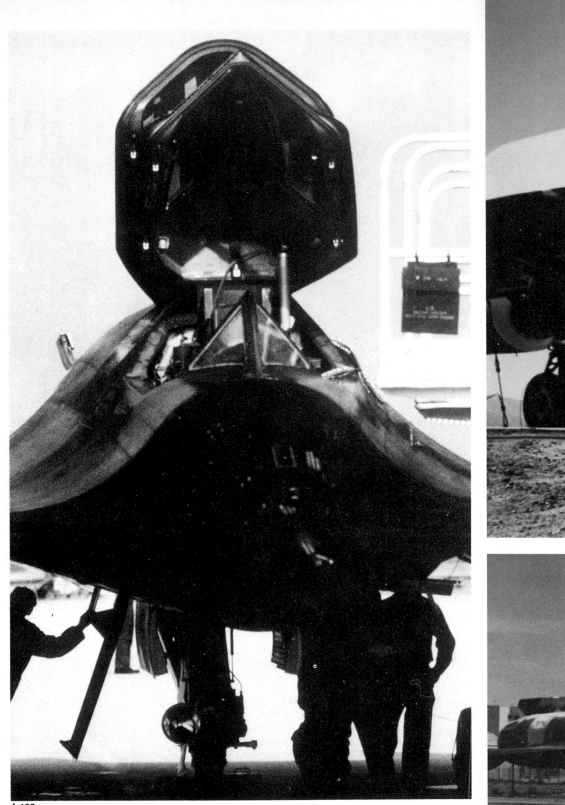

▲123

123. Different nose fixtures are attached to the fuselage, depending on the type of mission being flown. Note the contrast in black finishes. (Author)

124. A ground-level view of two A-12 aircraft in storage at Palmdale. An A-12 two-seat trainer is in the background. (Andrews)

125. A detailed look at the 'Titanium Goose', the two-seat A-12 trainer 06927. This aircraft appears in the Groom Lake group photo. (Andrews)

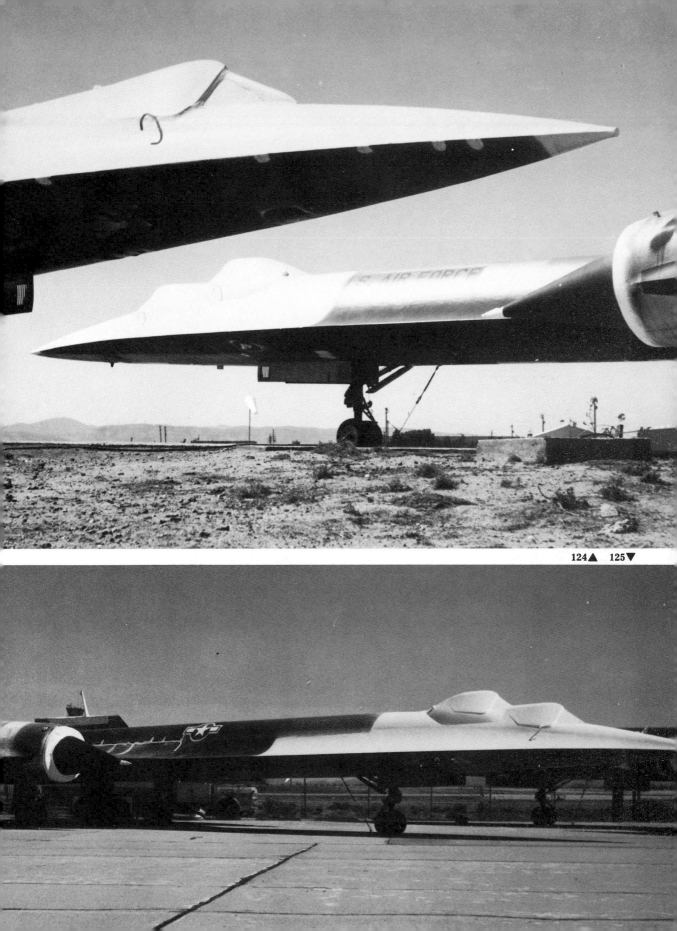

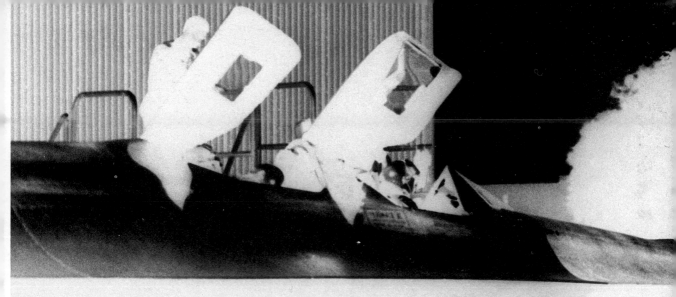

126. A declassified test photograph of Lockheed's Palmdale facility, taken from a U-2 at approximately 70,000ft; note the A-12 aircraft in 'mothball' storage. Two grey-camouflaged U-2C aircraft are visible, as is the fuselage of a U-2R extending out of the main hangar. (Goodall Collection)

127. The flight crew of the SR-71 consists of a pilot/commander and a Reconnaissance Systems Officer (RSO). Note the difference in reflectivity between the fuselage and nose attachment. (Author)

127 ▲

128. The first YF-12A takes off from Edwards AFB, California, during the mid-1960s Air Force flight test programme. The nacelle pods contained cameras to record weapons separation tests. (Lockheed)

128 ▼

129. YF-12A 06935 carries the 'Coldwall experiment', as part of the joint Air Force/NASA supersonic flight test programme. (NASA)

130. Aircraft 06935, in NASA markings, taxis on to the main runway at Edwards AFB in March 1979. (Author)

131. An SR-71B trainer preparing to taxi at Lockheed's Palmdale facility. Note the additional fins below the nacelles. (Lockheed)
132. An early 1960s photograph of YF-12A 06935 on the main ramp at the Groom Lake test facility. (Goodall Collection)

131▶

▼132

▲133 ▼134

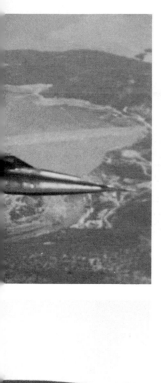

133. SR-71 17958 on a training flight from Beale AFB. All SR-71 aircraft at Beale belong to the 9th Strategic Reconnaissance Wing (SRW). (Lockheed)

134. Traffic stops because of a 'necessary' low approach to Wright-Patterson AFB, 7 November 1979. Aircraft 06935, devoid of NASA markings, makes its last landing prior to being placed on permanent display at the Air Force Museum as the sole surviving YF-12A. (Lockheed)

135. The cockpit of Lockheed YF-12A 06935 as it is seen today at the Air Force Museum, Wright-Patterson AFB, Ohio. (Andrews)

▲136

136. On the Advanced Development Projects drawing boards at Lockheed is a Mach 5 (3,500mph) aircraft capable of sustained 120,000ft flight. (Lockheed)

137. Low-observable 'stealth' technology is incorporated into the shape and structure of this future design. The aircraft would be capable of strike/penetration or reconnaissance missions. (Author)

▼137